Hate and Discrimination
in America

Hate and Discrimination in America

Lawrence J. King

Boulder, Colorado

Library of Congress Control Number: 2010902691
ISBN: Hardcover   978-1-4500-5206-1
                 Softcover   978-1-4500-5205-4
                 Ebook   978-1-4500-5207-8

To order additional copies of this book, contact:
Xlibris Corporation
1-888-795-4274
www.Xlibris.com
Orders@Xlibris.com
77232

CONTENTS

ACKNOWLEDGEMENTS

Special thanks to Donna Ann King, Tammy King Johnson, Gary Johnson, Terri King Porter, Billy Porter, Jane Figueroa, Luis Figueroa, Rebecca Ann King, Lawrence J. King, Jr., Rose Nardi, James Freedom Powell, Julia Gibbs, Brian Ridley, Robert Brown, Derek Santa, Sharon Santa, Jeffrey Muniz, Gary Allen, Margot Neuman, Jim Grady, Steve Duarte, Ralph Koteen, Peggy Heit, Kurt Foster, Sylvia Wagner, the Boulder Colorado police department, the Colorado Department of Corrections, Judge Dennis Maes, Gail Christonson, Sue Wick, Cheryl Holden, Adam Nunn, Tony Ferrano, Luis Arguillo, Amy Geithman, Kerry Lujan, Judy Lujan, James Blazon, Harold Alee, and all of the crew at Saxy's Café for having inspired me to write this book.

INTRODUCTION

In making this book it was not my intention to point a finger at any particular race, creed, color, gender or ethic group. I also do not wish to spread hate or to discriminate against anyone.

My objective is to point out some of the problems in our modern American day society and in the world, for that matter, in the hopes that people will better understand each other and be willing to deal with, simply put, right from wrong issues.

There is nothing wrong with being proud of who you are, where you come from, or even whom you choose to worship but there is everything wrong when you or any group of people like you choose to spread hate and to discriminate against others simply because they are different from that of who you are and/or what you represent.

This book is about acceptance, tolerance, and coexistence for the sake of humanity and a better world.

Lawrence J. King
Boulder, Colorado

PREAMBLE TO THE CONSTITUTION OF THE UNITED STATES OF AMERICA

We the people of the United States of America, in order to form a more perfect union, establish justice, ensure domestic tranquility, provide for common defense, promote the general welfare, and secure the blessing of liberty to ourselves and our posterity, do ordain and establish this constitution of the United States of America.

FOREWORD

Hate and Discrimination are spreading out of control in this country, and we need to put a stop to it. Yellow, Brown, Black, or White matters not, we all bleed red. In order for us to coexist together in harmony we must realize that there is no master race.

Rankism is usually associated with the thought process that causes one to hate and discriminate against others, mainly because of race, color, creed, political views, and language preferences.

Rankism means thinking that you are better than everyone else. The message is quite clear.

You and your actions affect the world around you. If we are truly to help one another and protect this home of ours, each of us needs to experience and develop a strong sense of compassion and responsibility towards each other.

Only these feelings can remove the self-centered motives that cause people to deceive and misuse one another. We need to do away with hate and discrimination and create a balance and bring about needed change for a brighter future and a better world.

WORD DEFINITIONS FROM WEBSTER'S NEW WORLD DICTIONARY OF THE AMERICAN LANGUAGE COLLEGE EDITION

HATE: To have strong dislike or ill will for; loathe; despise and or look down upon with great contempt toward the person or thing one hates.

DISCRIMINATION: A showing of difference or favoritism in treatment.

PREJUDICE: A judgment or opinion formed before the facts are known, a preconceived idea favorable or, more usually, unfavorable.

DESPISE: To look down on, be contemptuous or disdainful of.

INTOLERANT: Unwilling to tolerate others' opinions, or religious beliefs.

BIGOT: A person who holds a prejudice against a racial or religious group.

BIGOTED: Narrow-minded and intolerant. Obstinate, irrational, and with animosity towards others with different opinions.

CO-EXIST: To exist together at the same time, or in the same place.

TOLERANCE: Freedom from bigotry or prejudice.

HARMONY: Peaceable or friendly relations.

UNITY: Implies the oneness as in spirit, aims, interests, feeling, of that which is made up of diverse elements or individuals.

LOVE: The feeling of benevolence and brotherhood that all people should have toward each other no matter what race, creed or color you belong to.

HATE AND DISCRIMINATION IN AMERICA

This country is still one of the greatest countries in the entire world. America was founded on the principles of freedom to worship whomever you chose to call your higher power, the freedom of speech, and the right to keep and bear arms. (The land of the free and the home of the brave.)

The common belief is that if you apply yourself regardless of race, creed or color, you can rise to the top and in the pursuit of health and happiness, achieve your American dream. This idea sounds good, but unfortunately the reality in some cases is often not the case due to an existing problem of hate or discrimination in this country—which causes certain select individuals to fall short of the American dream.

The message is quite clear that you and your actions affect the world around you—so why spread hate and discontent when you can spread compassion, kindness, tolerance, and co-existence toward people who are different from you or what you represent.

What goes around comes around, so if you project hate and discriminate toward others, then one day you will experience hate and discrimination being projected right back at you.

All of the different religious faiths—despite their philosophical differences—have a similar objective. Every religion emphasizes human improvement, love, respect for others, and sharing other peoples' suffering. Along these lines every religion has more or less the same view point and the same goal.

SPECIAL REPORTS

The following information is from The Southern Poverty Law Center, Spring 2009 Volume 39, Number 1 and the Special Issue Intelligence Report Magazine Spring and Summer Editions 2009.

Recession creates a perfect storm and Obama may have smashed the ultimate political barrier for African Americans, but his presidency and the recession are creating a perfect storm for white supremacists intent on swelling their ranks.

Barack Obama's election has inflamed racist extremists who see it as another sign that their country is under siege by non-whites.

The idea of a black man in the White House combined with the economic crisis and continuing high levels of Latino immigration have given white supremacists a real platform on which to recruit.

Many hate groups agree that President Obama will be a visual aid for angry white Americans and could provoke a backlash among relatively mainstream whites, resulting in a dramatic increase in the ranks of extremists.

It would appear that the United States of America is turning once again into a "hater" nation. America currently has 926 registered hate groups.

The nation's top 5 hate group's hot spots are California, Florida, South Carolina, Georgia, and Tennessee, followed by New Jersey and Virginia tied for sixth place having 34 hate groups within their borders.

Hate groups are categorized as the Ku Klux Klan, Neo-Nazi, White Nationalist, Racist Skin Head, Christian Identity, Neo-Confederate, Black Separatist—to name a few—in addition to general hate groups.

General hate groups embrace ideologies of hatred. These include the sub-categories of Anti-Gay groups, anti-immigrant groups, Holocaust Denial groups, Racist Music labels, Radical Traditionalist Catholic groups and a variety of other groups endorsing a hodge—podge of hatred doctrines.

INTELLIGENCE REPORTS PUBLISHED BY THE SOUTHERN POVERTY LAW CENTER ISSUE 124, SUMMER 2009

Wichita, Kansas January 3, 2009

A cross and a wheel chair ramp were burned in the front yard of a couple that helps trouble youths.

Baton Rouge, Louisiana January 21, 2009

A noose was found on the desk of a black supervisor and another black employee at the governor's Office of Homeland Security and Emergency Preparedness.

Metairie, Louisiana March 10, 2009

A sign reading "KKK" was left in a black woman's front yard.

Camarillo, California January 5, 2009

Swastikas and anti-Semitic messages were etched on a Jewish preschool for the second time in a week.

Hartselle, Alabama January 19, 2009

A confederate battle flag was tied to a pole in front of predominantly black church.

Los Angeles, California February 13, 2009

A group of about 20 Hispanic youths allegedly attacked a black minister and his sons.

Malibu, California January 16, 2009

Swastikas, sexual symbols and crosses were sprayed on the walls, doors and windows of a Jewish center and synagogue.

Norfolk, Virginia January 19, 2009

Neo-Nazi fliers questioning the legitimacy of Barack Obama's presidency were left on vehicles.

Seattle, Washington January 6, 2009

Letters threatening attacks were sent out to 11 gay bars.

Fond du Lac, Wisconsin January 8, 2009

Racist cards were left on several car windows of people participating in a diversity event celebrating Latino heritage in the city.

Wildwood, Pennsylvania February 11, 2009

The condo of the only black man in a vacation complex was set afire two weeks after it was spray painted with racist graffiti.

Pittsburgh, Pennsylvania January 2, 2009

An Islamic center was vandalized.

Roosevelt, New York March 8, 2009

Four Latino men were arrested for allegedly attacking a black man with baseball bats while yelling racial slurs.

Sloatsburg, New York March 28, 2009

Five white teenagers were charged with assault as a hate crime after they allegedly beat a Latino teen while yelling "White Power!"

Portland, Oregon March 26, 2009

Three Native Americans—a man and two women—were beaten as they waited for a train, allegedly by three men and two women who used anti-Native American slurs.

Minneapolis, Minnesota January 22, 2009

A woman was allegedly assaulted by two men who shouted derogatory comments about her sexual orientation.

Rochester, Minnesota March 22, 2009

A 25 year old white man was charged with second degree assault for allegedly stabbing a black man with a screw driver while making racial slurs.

Billings, Montana January 8, 2009

A white supremacist flier was left at a church that supports the gay, lesbian, bisexual, and transgender community. Hate mail was also sent to the church.

IMPORTANT RECENT LEGISLATION THAT ADDRESSES HATE CRIMES

Matthew Shepard and James Byrd, Jr. Hate Crimes Prevention Act 2009

Public Law No. 111-84

After more than a decade of advocacy by the Human Rights Campaign, the Matthew Shepard and James Byrd, Jr. Hate Crimes Prevention Act (HCPA) was signed into law by President Barack Obama on October 28, 2009.

Wikipedia provides the following information on the background of this hate crimes legislation.

The Act is named after two victims of bias-motivated crimes in the United States, Matthew Shepard and James Byrd, Jr.

Matthew Shepard was a student who was tortured and murdered in 1998 near Laramie, Wyoming because he was perceived to be gay. His killers were not charged under hate crime laws because at the time the hate crime law in Wyoming did not recognize gay people as a suspect class.

James Byrd, Jr. was an African-American man who was tied to a truck by two known white supremacists, dragged, and decapitated in Jasper, Texas in 1998. Similarly, there was no hate crimes law in Texas at the time.

These murders and subsequent trials brought national and international attention to the need to amend U.S. hate crime legislation.

What is a Hate Crime? (From The Human Rights Campaign Nov. 10 2009)

A hate crime occurs when the perpetrator of a crime intentionally selects a victim because of who the victim is. Hate crimes rend the fabric of our society and fragment communities because they target an entire community or group of people, not just the individual victim.

The Hate Crimes Prevention Act gives the Department of Justice the power to investigate and prosecute bias-motivated violence by providing this agency with jurisdiction over crimes of violence where a perpetrator has selected a victim because of the person's actual or perceived race, color, religion, national origin, gender, sexual orientation, gender identity or disability.

In addition, it provides the Department of Justice with the ability to aid state and local jurisdictions with investigations and prosecutions of bias-motivated crimes of violence.

The Hate Crimes Prevention Act authorizes the Department of Justice to provide grants to state and local communities to cover the extraordinary expenses associated with the investigation and prosecution of hate crimes. It also authorizes the provision of grants for local programs to combat hate crimes committed by juveniles, including programs that train local law enforcement officers in identifying, investigating, prosecuting and preventing hate crimes.

Furthermore, the Hate Crimes Prevention Act requires the Federal Bureau of Investigation to track statistics on hate crimes based on gender and gender identity (statistics for the other groups were already tracked.)

INSIGHT ON THE TYPES OF PEOPLE WHO COMMIT HATE CRIMES

Research conducted by Levin and McDevitt of Northeastern University's Institute on Race and Justice shows that there are three major types of hate crime offenders:

- "Thrill seekers" who look for excitement and power in attacking a person they perceive as different.
- "Retaliators" who seek revenge for a real or perceived crime against someone similar to the attacker.
- "Defenders" who are trying to protect their neighborhood or way of life.

Perhaps the most expected type is also the rarest: an offender who may be a member of a known or unknown hate group and who has a deep-seated hatred toward a specific ethnic group.

"Hate criminals, most of them young men, believe they are carrying out the fervent, unspoken wishes of their communities," said Mark Potok, director of the Southern Poverty Law Center's Intelligence Report.

McDevitt says offenders often "believe other people share their biases . . . everybody feels the way they do, or at least the majority." By taking action, he says, they think "they're being heroic while others are scared."

CAUSE AND CONDITION

One of the reasons behind the hate and discrimination that have spread across this country is the outsourcing of American jobs to workers in other countries.

Another reason is because foreigners are now showing up in this country to get a piece of the American Dream and are willing to work for cheaper wages.

From a business perspective, it makes perfect sense. Having people work for you for less money creates greater profit. Isn't that the way that America works? (The premise of capitalism.)

Because of this philosophy and the reasons stated above, the average American worker who once upon a time long, long ago made good wages and had a comfortable life, is now seeing his or her job opportunities slip away. That situation is causing a lot of conflict, tension, fear, and discontent in the minds of the American people who were born and raised in the United States.

These conditions are conducive to hate and discrimination being projected toward people from other countries who now reside in the U.S.A.

PARTIAL SOLUTION

Skin color, language barriers, religious beliefs, political views, music, and gender preferences are often the reasons that people cannot coexist together.

Mainly and mostly the language barrier is what causes fear and problems—especially when people from other countries come to the United States and are not willing to learn or speak the English language. That being said, it is a mandatory requirement before any person from another country is allowed to become a U.S. citizen that they are required by law to pass an English exam.

By using the English language, people from different backgrounds would earn more respect, be better able to communicate more effectively with other nationalities, and to coexist more harmoniously together.

People come to this country searching for a better way of life; there is nothing wrong with that equation.

Diversity is good; we were all made different. If we were all the same, then life would be extremely boring.

Yellow, Brown, Black or White matters not. We all bleed red. In order for us to all get along we must all realize that there is no "Master Race".

Hate and discrimination issues are spreading out of control in this country, and we need to put a stop to it for the sake of a brighter future and a better world.

John Lennon said it in one of his songs, "All we are saying is give peace a chance."

HISPANIC/LATINO PEOPLE

Known for their wonderful variety of awesome foods such as tacos, burritos, enchiladas, quesadillas, and other delicious dishes, Latinos are also known to be very hard working people with loving and close-knit families.

However, a recent influx of illegal immigrants crossing over into this country from south of the border has a lot of Americans concerned as well as puzzled. FBI statistics show that anti-Latino crimes are on the rise. There were 595 anti-Latino crimes in 2007, up almost 40 percent from the 426 crimes in 2003; the Latino population in America grew only 14 percent during that time.

Some Americans think that these illegals are criminals because the news talks about Latino gang violence drive by shootings and other criminal activities almost on a daily basis.

Americans are asking themselves, "Are they going to take our jobs? They can't even speak English and are not willing to learn how to speak English, so why should they be allowed to live in this country?"

A lot of Americans are misinformed about Hispanic people. Some U.S. citizens commonly believe that the Hispanic/Latino people come to this country and live 10 deep in a house, work for cheap wages, take Americans jobs, and don't pay any taxes.

Furthermore, many people think that the Latinos cause a lot of problems because of their lack of wanting to learn or willingness to speak English.

These are some of the reasons for the hate and discrimination against the Hispanic/Latino people. Maybe the U.S. public needs to better inform themselves about the Hispanic/Latino people instead of being so judgmental. U.S. citizens should be grateful that Latinos are taking low paying jobs that many U.S. citizens don't want but are necessary to keep the economy running.

The U.S.A. has had many waves of immigrants in its history and each group has faced intense discrimination. One only has to look back 150 years to the way that the Irish, Polish and Italian immigrants were treated to see similarities with how we view Hispanics today. Obviously, we haven't learned from the past.

BLACK PEOPLE

Most African Americans or Black peoples' history is rooted in slavery. In 1865, the final step was taken in an amendment to the constitution which prohibited slavery anywhere in the United States. But it was not until the civil rights movement of the 1960s that the issue of racial equality was property addressed.

Historically, lynching was a system of punishment used by Europeans against African American slaves. In 1837 the editor of a paper was killed by a white mob after he published articles criticizing lynching and advocating the abolition of slavery. From 1889 through 1930 three thousand, seven hundred twenty-four people were lynched in the United States and four-fifths of those lynched were Negroes. (Dr. Arthur Raper report on lynching.) There were numerous attempts to pass a law in Congress to prohibit lynching, but none was successful.

Billie's Holiday's famous song, "Strange Fruit" was composed by Abel Meeropol (aka Lewis Allan—a school teacher who was extremely upset after seeing a picture of a Black man who was lynched.)

STRANGE FRUIT

Southern trees bear strange fruit
Blood on the leaves
Blood at the root
Black bodies swinging in the southern breeze
Strange fruit hanging from the poplar trees
Pastoral scene of the gallant south
The bulging eyes and the twisted mouth
The scent of magnolia sweet and fresh
Then the sudden smell of burning flesh
Here is a fruit for the crows to pluck
for the rain to gather
for the wind to suck
for the sun to rot
for the tree to drop
Here is a strange and bitter crop.

Even to this day, Black men and women are discriminated against, especially in the southern states. Hate crimes towards Blacks are on the rise.

We now have a Black president, Barack Obama. The people of the United States have spoken. Hopefully he can get the message across to the American people so everyone will stop hating and discriminating, and we can better coexist as a country at peace with itself.

Booker T. Washington once said, "You measure the size of the accomplishment by the obstacles you had to overcome to reach your goals."

Martin Luther King once said, "Free at last, free at last, thank God Almighty, free at last!"

He also said, "I have a dream that one day all of God's children, Black men and White men, Jews and Gentiles, Protestants and Catholics will harmonize upon the song of freedom."

WHITE PEOPLE

A lot of white U.S. citizens feel as if the U.S.A. is being overtaken by foreigners, and that what was once a minority is now becoming a majority. This attitude can create insecurity and fear, and—as a consequence—various pro-white groups are increasing in number.

In extremists' eyes, they see White as White and Black as Black; Brown as Brown; there is no gray area.

For many years in this country, discrimination and hatred have been projected upon minorities, and now it appears that in some cases, reverse discrimination is becoming a popular discussion. Certain instances have been reported and documented to this fact of the matter.

The Dalai Lama said it best when he said, "We must find a way to present basic human values to everyone—and present them not as religious matters but as secular ethics that are essential whether you are religious or not. Love for others and respect for their rights and dignity no matter who or what they are. So long as we practice this in our daily lives, no matter if we are learned or unlearned, whether we believe in Buddha or God, or follow some other religion or none at all, as long as we have compassion for others and conduct ourselves with restraint out of a sense of responsibility, there is no doubt we will be able to coexist in peace and harmony."

It does not matter what the color of your skin is. It matters how you act and interact with others and toward others.

NATIVE AMERICAN INDIANS

This ethnic group has been hated and discriminated against since the Europeans discovered America. The Native American Indians lived in this country long before any White man, Black man or Hispanic man ever did. If this country belongs to anyone, it would be the Native American Indian.

To look at their history once "the Europeans" (the early White settlers) appeared on the scene is shocking. The US government committed atrocities and genocide against the Native people for the purpose of obliterating them in order to take claim to their lands. Deliberately spreading diseases by giving them blankets that had been used by small pox victims, marching them several thousand miles without adequate provisions or rest so that many thousands died along the way ("The Trail of Tears"), and herding millions of buffalo (the Native Peoples' primary source of food, clothing and shelter) over cliffs to their deaths were but a few of the deliberate efforts to eliminate the Native Americans.

After many brutal marches and battles and the losses of many thousands of lives, the Native American Indians were put on reservations in the middle of deserts. Their livelihood was denied, alcohol became an everyday escape from the sad reality of their lives. Their children were forcibly removed from the reservations, sent to "Christian" boarding schools where they were brutally and cruelly denied their heritage. When the children returned to their homes, they did not fit in to either culture and had a very difficult time in both worlds.

As the great bison herds dwindled during the 1800s, many Native Americans turned to the new Ghost Dance religion, believing it would bring back the buffalo, resurrect the dead, and get rid of the White people. This religion came from the Piute prophet called Wovoka. Some believed that Wovoka was the Christ of whom missionaries had spoken, and many adopted his Ghost Dance, an event that is now recognized as a tribal holiday by the Oglala Sioux Nation. Whites felt threatened by the Ghost Dancers and this tension led to the massacre at Wounded Knee, South Dakota on December 29, 1890.

As a result of the demoralizing state of existence on the reservations—having had everything taken away from them by the White culture—Native peoples today suffer an extremely high unemployment rate, an astounding rate of alcoholism, very high rates of diseases, particularly diabetes and obesity, and domestic violence.

To this day, Native American Indians are still discriminated against and have not been compensated for what is rightfully theirs.

More than one hundred years ago, for example, the U.S. government set up a trust fund for the Native Americans. The purpose of the trust fund was to compensate them for the mineral rights on their lands that Whites appropriated. The US government, however, cannot determine how much should have been put into the trust fund initially; nor how much it should be worth today. The US government continues to discriminate against the Native Americans every chance it gets.

MY INTERVIEW WITH A WOMAN REGARDING HER PERSPECTIVE ON DISCRIMINATION AGAINST WOMEN

Most young women starting out today believe that the barriers and discrimination that women faced a generation ago are no longer around; that is, until they get serious about a career. Many view the previous generation of women who fought hard to crack the glass ceiling during the 1960s and early 1970s as strident feminists. And unfortunately, young women today are generally unappreciative of the efforts of women like Gloria Steinem and Betty Freidan from the 1960's who put forth strong, consistent and courageous effort to change the tide of history in order to gain rights for women.

As one woman said recently (NY Times Oct 2009), "My generation of professional women took equality for granted." Yet working women today stand on the shoulders of those feminist pioneers.

A generation ago when bright young women with business, finance or economic degrees applied for jobs the interviewer *legally* told them "We are not hiring women". In spite of a degree with honors from a highly regarded university, as a woman I was not even given the chance to interview with some companies because of their policy of not hiring women. Quickly learning to use my initials instead of my first name, I made it into the door of interviewers only to be told by a shocked man, "Oh, you're a woman!" Then he either said, "We're not hiring women" or "I don't know what to say to you; you're a woman."

Even though I told him I was serious about a job with his company (Ford Motor being one of those companies) and even though I had a great resume, the discussion about a potential job was never begun because of my not being male.

As one of less than a handful of women in many economics, finance and business classes, I was used to being in the minority, but I resented being singled out for mockery by male professors because I was a woman.

The university tolerated several professors who openly mocked the women in their classes. One professor of business law—a judge in Cleveland, Ohio at the time—made it a point to run every woman out of his classes year after year. He methodically started harassing one woman at a time until she couldn't take it any more and dropped the class. Year after year this pattern continued and his reputation was known. I was the last woman left out of a handful one semester who had enrolled in his business law class. I fully intended to be strong and fight it out, but eventually (after 2 weeks of harassment) I caved in. (I was only 20 years old and not yet steeled.) It came to the point of my feeling it wasn't worth it. It wasn't a required class and I would be graduating soon.

What galls me so much now is (1) The university had to be aware of his reputation and tolerated it year after year. (2) None of the male students in the class stood up for a woman's rights to take the business law class (3) Nor did any of the men say anything to the professor/judge about his unjust, unprofessional and discriminating behavior.

In the 1960—and early 1970's—men were used to having everything their way in school, careers and life. They were used to seeing women subjugated verbally and every other way.

A good female friend of mine made it through Case Western Reserve's rigorous pre-med classes and met with her advisor to discuss applying to med school. Her (male) advisor said he liked the idea of her getting an M.D. and commended her because "the medical profession needed secretaries who could understand medicine." This woman became a successful dermatologist in spite of her advisor and in spite of the difficulty women in medicine and other professions faced in that era.

A close family friend was a highly skilled female anesthesiologist (M.D.) in the 1980s—1990s and she, too, encountered constant gender discrimination in her practice. The male anesthesiologists were given the plum cases, operations and most desired work schedules. She was given the leftovers. She was taunted by her colleagues for being a rare female in a male dominated segment of medicine.

Another good female friend is an ER physician today, and she also finds regular discrimination in her work environment—again with regard to schedules and cases. She gets the "leftovers" and the work that the male ER docs don't want. So we certainly don't see as much progress in equal treatment over the past 40 years as we would have hoped to have.

A journalist who began her career in 1980 with the Wall Street Journal said that she and her professional female colleagues didn't discuss sexual harassment; that "was just a part of life". In 2008 13,867 charges of sexual harassment were reported to the Equal Employment Opportunity Commission with 16% filed by men, 84% by women. That is just the tip of the iceberg of harassment because much—if not most—goes unreported.

I personally have been subjected to numerous situations of discrimination and harassment by clients, colleagues and corporate leaders in my 25 year career. I reported some to my supervisor, and his response was the advice: "Deal with it!" I knew his response was morally, ethically wrong and illegal. Some I chose not to report, recognizing that pursuing the situation legally would cost me not only my job but probably any future jobs. When word reached our corporate attorney, his assistant told me his response was, "She is a big girl. She can take it." When I finally documented another outrageous harassment situation to the corporate attorney that took place with the harasser and my supervisor was present and laughed with him, actions were finally taken to remove me from the situation. And within a few months I was coincidentally demoted.

In a different setting today where women dominate the workforce because of the low wages that are paid, men are generally favored for promotion over women. One needs only to look at the top level personnel in most large retail businesses, financial services and education to see the dominance by mostly men and very few women.

In the 1970's, women earned 59 cents for every dollar that a man earned. In 1983 the amount increased to 64 cents. Today women still earn less than men: 77 cents for every dollar that a man earns (whether the woman had a college degree or a high school degree; the ratio is the same.) Even worse, the Shriver Report 2009 found that "Working mothers earn 15% less on average than men and single mothers earn 40% less."

Zookeepers make more than workers who care for children. What does that tell us about how society views the value of women?

Unfortunately, the pace of women's wage improvement has slowed. Studies have been done on the pay gap and a recent study Feb. 2007 by economists Blau and Kahn say that 41% of the pay gap is "unexplainable"—meaning not due to race, education, union membership, occupation and industry. That 41% is *not* unexplainable to women. We understand it: it is outright discrimination against females because they can get away with it. If all women went on strike for one week, the economy would come to a quick standstill and America would have a better perspective of the value of women's contributions. However, women are neither assertive enough nor united to accomplish this.

50% of all workers today are female. Mothers are the primary breadwinners in 4 of every 10 American families. (The Shriver Report 2009). A recent study documented that in a family where both the man and woman work outside the home, the woman puts in many more hours of housework than her partner or spouse. If there are children in the family, the woman again spends many more hours with childcare and child raising issues than the man. So the woman earns less working outside the home, then comes home and works harder and longer at home. And the phrase "Women are the weaker sex" still persists in spite of the reality of today's working world.

Do men have discussions to the same degree that women do about balancing work and family?

Contributing factors include the facts that women *will* work for less; women do not ask for raises the way men do; single women need jobs to support their families and there are many single women and single mothers; there are no "old girl" networks the way that there are "old boy" networks. These networks are key to having mentors and sponsors that can help with developing one's career.

Our workforce and education system is still segregated, steering women into low-paid, low-status, low-security professions. The fact that men have not integrated to any large degree the female dominated professions reflects the perceived lower status and lower pay and fewer benefits of those jobs traditionally held by women.

The Shriver Report (2009) documents that "A woman who goes to the same kind of school, gets the same grades, has the same major, takes the same kind of job and has the same personal characteristics as her male colleague earns 5% less the first year out of school. The gender pay gap accumulates over time."

The Center for American Progress found that the cumulative pay gap over 40 years saw women lose an average of $434,000 in income compared to men. The pay gap accumulates for a number of reasons, but importantly, pay raises are typically given as a percentage of one's annual salary. So if your salary is always lower, pay raises will be always be lower. The Shriver Report documents that "women with the same degrees still lag behind men's pay and almost never catch up. Education raises women's pay, but the gender gap remains at all educational levels."

The Shriver Report also found that "Job candidates identified as mothers were perceived to be less competent, less promotable, less likely to be recommended for management, less likely to be recommended for hire, and had lower recommended starting salaries" than identical males. "The job candidates identified as fathers were not penalized in the same way, and often saw a boost."

Woman's gains in corporate America stalled after 1985: the same number of board seats; the same number of corporate officer positions. In 2008 women made up half of all law firm associates but only 18% of partners. Yet, the Shriver Report found that "Companies that consistently promote women to positions of power and leadership over time and across their operations have greater financial success across a variety of measures."

During the 2008 presidential primaries, the topic of race was not discussed. One would hardly know from reading the news or listening to the radio that one of the candidates was black. However, Hillary's gender and comments on her appearance and behavior were not off the table for discussion, including disrespectful and insulting comments.

The media's handling of women in the last several years has deteriorated; there is far less respect as evidenced by Keith Olbermann of MSNBC calling Michelle Balkin, the conservative blogger, "a big mashed up bag of meat with lipstick on it" or Glenn Beck of Fox News suggesting that "ugly women" are probably "progressive as well". (Joann Lipman "The Mismeasure of Woman" the New York Times, Oct. 24, 2009.) The media continues to present unrealistic images of women, focusing on glamour, power, and sex.

Women face discrimination in the area of health insurance as well. Women pay more for their health insurance and have more unique forms of discrimination in their coverage. Did you know that "domestic violence" is a pre-existing condition in health insurance?

Another form of discrimination against women is the fact that Insurance companies charge women more than men for the same exact coverage. Most Americans believe that it is illegal today for employers to fire a pregnant worker, but that is not the case. (Shriver Report 2009) Even if a doctor provides documentation that a pregnant patient should be put on a lighter work load (e.g., less heavy lifting), an employer is not required to transfer the pregnant woman to a different job where there is less lifting and the employer can legally fire her.

While an Equal Rights Amendment never passed Congress, other laws have been passed that give women more rights than they had prior to the efforts of the 1960's feminists. Although the United States thinks of itself as an advanced country, we have only to look at the political make up of other countries governing bodies to see how many more women hold in public office throughout the world. Many countries around the world now have and have had female leaders even as far back as decades ago. (Margaret Thatcher, Golda Meir, Indira Gandhi).

Government policies and laws are still based on an outdated model of the American family. The United States is still the only major industrialized nation without comprehensive child care and family leave policies.

What do women want? Freedom, opportunity, respect, dignity, self-determination and equality.

PEOPLE FROM THE MIDDLE EAST

Long before 9/11, people from the Middle East were frequently victims of discrimination. Since the days of 9/11, people from the Middle East are sometimes even hated because they have, for the most part, been given the label of "Terrorists".

Following 9/11, people from the Middle East have been subject to hate crimes and are commonly discriminated against.

Anyone can be classified as a terrorist, especially if he or she does not believe in what you believe in. So why is it that people in America who came here from the Middle East have been given the name of and stamped with the label of "Terrorist"?

Because of the propaganda that has been spread against them by the media: radio, television, newspapers, etc. Now anyone in America who came from the Middle East is being held accountable and responsible for the attack on the Twin Towers. Simply sharing the same birthplace as those who attacked the Twin Towers does not make everyone from the Middle East a terrorist.

Can we stop the madness?

ORIENTAL/ASIAN PEOPLE

Sometimes thought of as mysterious, Asian people have been in this country for a long time. In U.S. history books they are best known for building the railroads across the continent in the 1800's. Had it not been for their almost slave labor, this country would not have expanded westward at the fast rate that it did; California would not have been settled, and the gold rush wouldn't have taken place. As the Chinese workers built the railroads, however, they were treated extremely badly by the White race.

The Asian Nation website provides the following information:

Blatant discrimination is documented centuries ago with US federal law: *The Chinese Exclusion Act of 1882.* For the first and so far only time in American history, an entire ethnic group was singled out and forbidden to step foot on American soil. Although this was not the first such anti-Asian incident, it symbolizes the legacy of racism directed against Asians.

This law was followed by numerous denials of justice against Chinese and Japanese immigrants seeking to claim equal treatment to land ownership, citizenship, and other rights in state and federal court in the early 1900s. Many times, Asians were not even allowed to testify in court. Perhaps the most infamous episode of anti-Asian racism was the unjustified imprisonment of Japanese Americans during World War II—done solely on the basis of their ethnic ancestry.

The last 20 years has seen Asian Americans become the fastest-growing targets for hate crimes and violence. Combined with the cultural stereotype of Asian Americans as quiet, weak, and powerless, more and more Asian Americans are victimized, solely on the basis of being an Asian American.

Perhaps the most graphic and shocking incident that illustrates this process was the murder of Vincent Chin in 1982. Vincent was beaten to death by two White men (Ronald Ebens and Michael Nitz) who called him a "Jap" (even though he was Chinese American) and blamed him and the Japanese auto-makers for the recession and the fact that they were about to lose their jobs. After a brief scuffle inside a local bar/night club, Vincent tried to run for his life until he was cornered nearby, held down by Nitz while Ebens repeatedly smashed his skull and bludgeoned him to death with a baseball bat.

The equally tragic part of this murder was how Vincent's murderers were handled by the criminal justice system. First, instead of being put on trial for second degree murder (intentionally killing someone but without premeditation), the prosecutor instead negotiated a plea bargain for reduced charges of manslaughter (accidentally killing someone). Second, the judge in the case sentenced each man to only two years probation and a $3,700 fine—and absolutely no jail time at all.

In the early 1900's, Japanese farmers came to America and brought superior farming techniques and a very strong work ethic. Many settled in the Pacific Northwest, not far from where they landed, and established fertile fruit farms—particularly in Oregon. White Americans were jealous of the Japanese farmers' success and prosperity and used the bombing of Pearl Harbor as an excuse to remove the Japanese—many of whom were American citizens by birth—from their property and send them to concentration camps in the United States. The camps were like animal pens with sub-human living conditions. When the war was over and the Japanese Americans returned to their former homes, few found them in the condition they were left. Much of their property had been outright stolen by neighbors and others. Today as you travel through the fertile fruit orchards and lavender fields around Hood River, Oregon or the lovely upscale community on Bainbridge Island, remember how those beautiful areas were stolen from their owners.

Some Americans today have a zero tolerance level for the current Chinese government because of decades of human rights violations in China and in Tibet. Tiananmen Square is probably the most famous human rights violence in recent memory. With regard to Tibet, the Chinese government caused the Dali Lama to leave his home and forced him into exile. The Chinese government is systematically destroying the Tibetan way of life similar to the way that the White man did to the Native American Indian.

Historically, Asians have a long history of conflict with Americans: World War II when the Japanese bombed Pearl Harbor, the Viet Nam war, and even now with North Korea building nuclear bombs. Some of the reason for the ongoing discrimination could be that many Americans have not yet healed and have many wounds from the past wars that have scared so many peoples' souls. Can we let go of the past so we can co-exist together for a better tomorrow?

GAY PEOPLE

Gay rights have come a long way but still have a long way to go in order for J.P. Public to accept and tolerate same sex relationships. One reason behind this ever so different and complicated topic is because of the opinions and beliefs that certain people have.

I have often heard people say, "God made Adam and Eve, not Adam and Steve." This statement alone is discriminating against gay people, but, unfortunately, some of mainstream America and a lot of the mainstream religions are anti-gay. Close minded people will state that being gay is legally and immorally wrong. My assessment of the situation would be to live and let live because what people do behind closed doors is no one else's business.

Whom you choose to share your life with is up to you. God said, love thy neighbor as thyself and do unto others as you would have them do unto you.

For Christ's sake, can't we all just get along?

LESBIAN PEOPLE

Many women these days are choosing to be lesbians. One reason could be because some women have been used and abused and mistreated by men. But also, it is very natural and normal physically and psychologically for some women without any history of abuse by men to prefer relationships with other woman.

Women who turn lesbian are sometimes seeking comfort and companionship in the arms of a woman because who better to understand the needs, desires, and everyday problems that a woman experiences. You guessed it: another woman. Just like some lesbians, some heterosexual men have turned gay because spouses, girlfriends, and

significant others have over stepped their boundaries and these men have been used and abused by their women partners.

Lesbians are often discriminated against by heterosexual women as well as by heterosexual men.

I have heard various people make fun of lesbians by saying lesbians are freaks, muff divers, and out there kind of people.

A lot of men say, "If a lesbian would go to bed with me, she would never think about being lesbian again." This arrogant comment is typical of a lack of understanding and definitely discrimination against lesbians.

These jokes and snide remarks of the most discriminating kind need to stop.

Women haters, men haters—who needs the drama? Coexistence is the only answer.

HOMELESS PEOPLE

Homeless people are often hated and discriminated against in this country, especially when it comes to finding gainful employment.

As soon as an employer or potential employer discovers that this particular individual is living at the local shelter or on the street, then he or she is either instantly fired or has no chance at all of landing a job.

All that is a sad statement of affairs because, for the most part, the homeless person has lost everything they own as a result of a tragic event in their life such as divorce, identity theft, medical expenses, prison or jail, accidents such as a car wreck, possible mental illness or some addiction problem.

The homeless person simply needs a helping hand so they can put their life back together. But as long as people continue to look down upon homeless people, then the homeless don't stand a chance in hell of making it back to the land of the living.

BIKERS/MOTORCYCLISTS

People that drive motorcycles do so for a lot of reasons: the feel of freedom as well as the fact that it is an effective and inexpensive means and way of getting from point A to point B. Also, there is a sense of community and belonging while in a large group of motorcyclists.

Bikers are often hated or discriminated against because some people have the misconception that all bikers are mean, tattooed criminals that have no respect for the law and constantly cause discontent wherever they go. In some cases this is true, but for the most part bikers today are in a class or league of their own and come from good backgrounds.

Bikers today are doctors, lawyers, judges, politicians, and policemen. These people are starting to find out what true freedom really is: the open road, the wind in your face and the rush of person and machine becoming one with all that is.

So the next time you see a group of bikers passing by don't be so quick to think negative thoughts about them.

PEOPLE WITH WEIGHT PROBLEMS

Frequently people who are over weight experience hate and discrimination from others.

Some over weight people are laughed at and ridiculed because of an eating disorder.

In a lot of cases, a person that is over weight is not totally responsible for his/her condition. Thyroid issues and gland problems are a major contributing factor to obesity.

People often think that because a person is overweight, they are naturally lazy people and do not care about their appearance.

As you can see, some medical conditions can be the cause and reason behind individuals being over weight. So therefore, don't be so quick to think badly about people with weight problems before you take a good look at yourself because we all have some kind of problem or issue to deal with.

PEOPLE WITH DISABILITIES

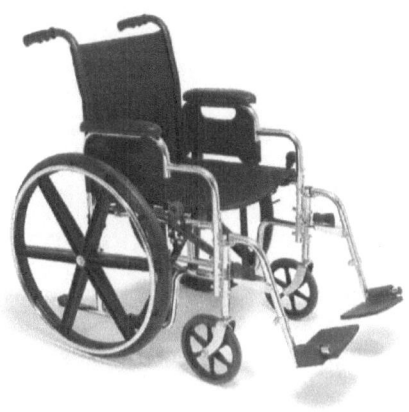

A woman who has a 40% disability in her hand and arm worked for a company without any problems for over a year. Everything was perfectly fine. She enjoyed what she was doing, was good at what she did, and her supervisor and co-workers were content and satisfied with her work. One day, however, the company changed store managers. The new manager did not like the disabled woman, so the supervisor changed the disabled woman's work load and schedule.

The new store manager told the disabled woman to perform different tasks that the manager knew would not be possible for the disabled woman to do. As a result, the disabled woman was terminated because of her inability to perform the required job.

This is a classic case of discrimination. The new store manager did not comply with laws that protect disabled workers; the company's human resource department should have educated the manager and corrected the situation. Instead the handicapped individual was fired after having worked satisfactorily for over a year.

No law suit was filed and the handicapped woman was not compensated for the loss of her job.

Because of the personal trauma to her confidence level and because of her disability, she never got up the courage to try to find gainful employment ever again.

Although there are laws to protect these handicapped individuals, oftentimes these things go unreported—causing devastating results like this to people with disabilities.

TATTOOS

Some employers will not allow people with visible tattoos to work for them. So therefore people who have visible tattoos are forced to cover them up.

If the tattooed person gets the job, then he or she is most likely to be put in the back of the business, away from the mainstream where all of the action takes place and away from attending to potential customers.

Tattoos are a form of artistic expression and should be seen as such, but unfortunately mainstream society often automatically thinks that tattooed individuals have criminal backgrounds—therefore discriminating against these people without even giving the tattooed person a chance.

EX-OFFENDERS

The latest hate and discrimination issues are being directed towards ex-sex offenders to the degree that as a group they are almost scared out of their minds. This fear is similar to what the Jewish people experienced under Adolf Hitler.

The media has spread hate all over this country and incites discrimination on almost a daily basis against ex-sex offenders.

In some cases, sex offenders are very dangerous people. However, once they paid their debt to society and want to get on the normal path, they should be allowed to gain their self respect back and not be stamped or labeled as an unpredictable time bomb just waiting for the chance to strike again.

The law requires ex-sex offenders to register quarterly after being released from prison. In some cases, ex-sex offenders must register with local law enforcement agencies for the remainder of their natural lives.

Until not long ago, they were required to register only once a year on their birthday and/or if they decided to move. However, the law changed so that now a quarterly registration is required for all ex-sex offenders, depending upon how serious their criminal act is rated.

This more frequent registration allows law enforcement the ability to track ex-sex offenders' whereabouts in order to further harass and intimidate these individuals. This harassment is clearly a human rights violation.

Once stamped as a sex offender, a person is treated as if he or she has the plague or some other kind of contagious disease because no one wants them around. This attitude comes from all the negative media publicity and hate propaganda that has spread all across this country about sex offenders.

For the most part, it's not the *registered* ex-sex offender that the public needs to worry about. It's the unregistered and undetected sex offender: the person who has not been caught—like someone's father, brother, sister, mother, cousin, aunt, uncle or neighbor. These are all possibilities of common sex offenders that haven't been uncovered.

Most sex offenders who have been caught have undergone extensive therapy to help them understand the seriousness of their problem as well as to rethink their way of thought and behavior process so as not to ever engage in this kind of behavior again.

Most therapists have the idea or misconception that this situation is not curable—but only treatable.

Why would therapists believe sex offenders could be cured? They would work themselves out of a job.

Ex-convicts, especially ex-sex offenders, have an extremely difficult time finding gainful employment, housing and social acceptance. Thus, they are usually destined to return to prison because either they are set up for some bogus crime or no one will give them the chance to prove themselves.

By all rights and all that's fair, once a person has paid his debt to society he (or she) should be allowed to have a fresh start to begin again in the pursuit of health, happiness and the American dream. Unfortunately, that is not the case. Ex-convicts/ex-sex offenders only want to forget about their past and return to being a productive member of society, but the stigma and stereotyping is enormous.

During my interviews with people who have been labeled by society as ex-murderers, ex-rapists, and ex-thieves I discovered that they all have one thing in common. Even though they paid their debt to society and served time in prison, and even though they are not bound by probation or parole, they are still hated and discriminated against.

Some of these individuals get lucky because they have somewhat of a support system in place. But for the most part, many return to prison because they don't stand a chance in hell of making it in modern day society once they have been labeled ex-convict or convicted felon or ex-sex offender.

If they tell the truth on a job application about being a convicted felon, then they usually do not find gainful employment. As a result, they are forced to lie on job applications just to get their foot in the front door of a business.

Once employed all goes well for a while, until it is discovered that they have a past record of criminal activity. The police sometimes show up at their workplace while checking up on their whereabouts, flashing the ex-convict's picture around and freaking everyone out. This leads to the ex-convict losing his or her job and the cycle repeats itself again: no job, no hope, no money, and no future.

Law enforcement agencies invade ex-offenders and ex-sex-offenders private lives by showing up at their homes and places of work. This very often causes the ex-offenders to lose their jobs, their homes, apartments and other living arrangements because the landlord or housing authority can't seem to deal with the stereotypical equation that states that all ex-offenders /sex offenders are dangerous and unpredictable people. This situation is the result of the media's portrayal and hype as well as Joe Policemen showing up, saying that he is trying to protect society from these individuals. That's straight up hate and discrimination.

This is total madness because society believes all of the propaganda that is being put before them by the media with regard to ex-offenders/ex-sex offenders.

Why does this continue to happen? Because these individuals do not have a voice or anyone to represent them, that's why.

The ex-convict remains separate and cut off from mainstream society, only wanting to get on with his or her life and to be able to become an outstanding (or normal) citizen again. But with no support system in place, the ex-convicts become easy prey to be set up by the police—or anyone else for that matter—for alleged crimes. They are often put back in jail before they even get a chance to prove themselves.

At this time there are approximately 900,000 sex offenders nation wide. Imagine if they were united as one strong group of people with the purpose of stopping this insane witch hunt; imagine if they marched on Washington D.C. to make the statement that they are tired of being harassed, hated and discriminated against. Their goal is to have the government put things in the proper perspective so that the ex-offenders can stop having their human rights violated. Then there could be a snowball's chance in hell of the ex-offender/ex-sex-offender making it in this country once again.

People should be forgiven for their mistakes and be allowed to move forward with their lives without a stamp or label associated with their past, once they've paid their debt to society. God Bless the U.S.A. Wake up America, before it's too late! If you don't wake up, sooner or later you, too, just might find yourself on the receiving end of hate and discrimination.

SOME OF THE REASONS EX-CONVICTS RETURN TO PRISON

(A) Upon release from prison, there is no support system in place. i.e. no family or friends because usually everyone that was in their life before they went to prison are now no longer apart of the person being released from prison's life.

(B) No Money. In prison the daily wage is 62 cents per day. Unless the released prisoner has managed to save a portion of that money over the years, upon release they are broke which causes a list of other problems like not being able to secure a place to live, or even be able to purchase food necessary to live.

(C) While in prison some convicts take medications for anxiety or stress related problems prescribed by the department of corrections physicians. Upon release the convict is so used to and/or dependent on those medicines that his or her body is in need of these medications and cannot function without them. Because the person being released from prison has no support system and probably no money, they can't purchase those needed medicines. That situation sets the stage for possibly new crimes so that the ex-convict can have his or her needed medications.

(D) Even if the released prisoner does have money, for the most part no one will allow them to purchase a place to live or establish a residence, all because of the media hype and stereotype against convicted felons and the "Oh My God approach" to "Sorry you are a convicted felon, but we don't want you around here because you are a bad person."

(E) Because of background checks most employers now days will not hire ex-convicts; or if they do choose to hire ex—convicts, it's usually a dead end job that leads to no where and causes the ex-convict to have stress, drama, and a lot of anger issues because with a dead-end job there is no way in hell they can achieve the American dream.

(F) Some ex-convicts purchase storage units and live out of an 8x12 enclosed space similar to a prison cell until the management finds out about it. Then it's the same old story all over again, which leads to back to prison for about 70% of the people who have been released from prison because No residence, No job, No support system in place, No money, and No hope of making it is a bad combination and usually ends with tragedy once again.

I am not saying feel sorry for these individuals who have made mistakes and poor choices in life, I am saying our current system and the mind set of some people in this country need to change so that ex-convicts will have an opportunity to prove that they are capable and worthy of being productive members of society once again if given the chance.

COFFEE SHOP HARASSMENT

A man was sitting in a coffee shop, working on his computer and drinking tea when all of a sudden he saw policemen swarming outside the coffee shop. About ten minutes later, two policemen came into the coffee shop and talked to one of the coffee shop personnel. They left the building and reappeared fifteen minutes later, entered the shop and approached the man who was working on his computer.

They asked him to step outside, which he did. The police began to search the man. They searched his back pack that he used to carry his computer, and they searched his leather jacket. The police found nothing—no weapons, no drugs, nothing.

After the police determined who the man was, they told him that someone had just attempted to rob the Subway sandwich shop next door, and the description that was given stated that the robber was wearing a bandana just like the patron of the coffee shop had on.

The patron was further detained until a new detective arrived. The detective looked at the detained man and said, "I'm the new guy." The detained man did not know what he meant by that until the new detective said, "I will see you on Wednesday." Then the detained man knew exactly what the detective meant. You see, the man who was removed from the coffee shop and questioned was a registered ex-sex offender/ex-convict, and he was scheduled to do his quarterly registration on Wednesday.

The detained man told the police that he had, in fact, eaten lunch at that Subway shop and if they wanted to walk with him to the Subway, he could produce witnesses to attest to the fact that he was not the robber. The police were not interested in checking that out and let the ex-sex offender go.

The ex-sex offender had to wonder, based on experience, was the Subway really the reason for being detained and questioned or was it a fabricated story by the police to determine the identity of the man working on the computer? You see, the homeless shelter is near this particular coffee shop, and the police often harass and detain people from the homeless shelter by going through their belongings to find out who these people are.

Needless to say, the ex-convict/registered ex-sex offender knew he was probably going to be arrested and set up for the attempted robbery at the Subway shop because that's how it usually works out.

Ex-convicts are harassed and sometimes have false charges put on them so the police can put these people back in jail.

And this is what needs to stop in this country: discrimination and harassment towards ex-convicts, especially when they've paid their debt to society.

DISCRIMINATION AGAINST EVERYONE

The minimum wage in the USA is better than it used to be; however, the cost of living has gone up and people who make minimum wage are still living in poverty.

America is a very rich country and is often called the land of opportunity. The government should first pass a bill to raise minimum wage to $10 per hour so that the average American citizen who is working for the minimum wage would have an opportunity to do more than just survive. The current minimum wage is still discriminating against poor people. Then the minimum wage should be indexed to inflation the same way that social security payments are indexed to inflation. That way, changes would be automatic and occur as needed (undoubtedly more frequently than they have in the past) since the government would not have to decide when to address the issue and to debate about it.

Congress votes itself salary increases more often than it adjusts the minimum wage so that the rich get richer and the poor stay poor. In 2009 Congress voted itself a 3% salary increase, a 0%

increase for social security, and no change in the minimum wage. Inflation was 0% in 2009, yet Congress looked out for its own self interest.

Another form of discrimination against everyone is the parking meter—taxation without representation. Why should we U.S. citizens pay money to come to town? That is absurd and, quite frankly, absolutely wrong. We all pay enough taxes as it is, without having to pay parking meters every time we come to town to go shopping, to the post office, or to other businesses.

If your meter expires and you don't get back in time to feed it, you receive a parking ticket: average cost = $15.00 per ticket. So why do we pay parking meters? So that towns and cities across this country can pay the meter maids so they can give you a ticket when the parking meter expires? What's wrong with this picture? Everything is wrong with this picture. Charging people to come to a shopping area is a deterrent. It makes towns and cities less inviting for people to come to; it makes it more challenging for businesses to attract shoppers.

HOUSEWIVES

Women who choose to stay home and take care of their families are never compensated for that work.

Let's say they do this job for thirty years. At the end of thirty years they do not receive a check from the government as the typical American worker does from his/her retirement plan or social security.

Maybe if the housewives would be compensated for cooking, cleaning, and other such chores then more women would choose to or could afford to stay home and take care of people they love.

Imagine this: if more women stayed at home to help and support their families, there would be more paying jobs in America—putting a dent in the current recession that this country is presently dealing with.

What a concept—what an idea. It sounds pretty good to me. Stay at home moms and wives would help boost the economy and possibly put this country on track economically and get paid in the process. Is this a fantasy? It could be a reality if our government would be open to this possibility.

HEALTH CARE WORKER

A man had worked more than a year with no problems whatsoever for an in-home health care company. He took care of mentally and physically challenged individuals.

When he was first hired by the company, the man showed the company solid references, having worked in this field for a long time. His references were outstanding.

His duties consisted of cooking, cleaning, light house keeping chores, laundry, and grocery shopping. He did all of these things letter perfect. In addition, he would go over and above his duties by taking his clients on little outings such as to the park, out to breakfast, lunch and dinner. He would play board games with his clients, hang out socializing and keeping them company. He even set up doctors appointments for his clients which were not a part of his job description—but he cared about his clients and wanted to help them as much as he could. Case in point, he went over and above the call of duty.

All of his clients loved him and were perfectly satisfied with him as a personal care provider. Furthermore, he was recognized by his company as employee of the month, received two awards (the WOW award and the Bright Light award), and he received a pay increase for a job well done.

One day a police officer showed up at the health care worker's main office and flashed the health care worker's picture all over, asking everyone in the office, "Does this man work here or for your organization? Did you know he is a registered sex offender?"

This action by the police officer caused a major drama at the office and for the registered ex-sex offender.

The health care worker was called in by his company and asked to explain the situation. He explained that his conviction dated back to 1997, approximately twelve years previously. The people at the office said they would try and talk to the key people in California and explain the health care worker's outstanding work history performance for the company. Hopefully, he would be able to keep his job.

A week later the health care worker was terminated from his job. The justification for his being fired was the "We can't allow you to work for us anymore because if we do, we could lose our business license."

This is another example of total discrimination and just plain wrong. That's why I say ex-convicts usually don't stand a chance of becoming a productive member of society again—often because the police continue to harass them even after the ex-convict has paid his debt to society.

SMOKERS VERSUS NON-SMOKERS

So many laws have been passed in this country that clearly discriminate against people who choose to smoke cigarettes, cigars, and pipes.

From a non-smoker's perspective, it's a matter of being subjected to breathing second hand smoke from people who choose to smoke. In some cases, second hand smoke has been reported to have caused cancer or other health related issues in people who do not smoke but who did breathe in second hand smoke.

It has been determined by the Surgeon General that smoking greatly increases your chance of health problems. However, to the active smoker, he or she feels that he or she should have the right and the opportunity to smoke wherever and whenever. Smoking for some people is an outlet and a way of relieving stress.

Some airports, government buildings, restaurants, coffee shops, hospitals, colleges, bus terminals, prisons, jails, and casinos have been declared off limits to smokers.

So tell me, who is really being discriminated against: the smoker or the non smoker? Maybe both.

PRIVATE PAY
DISCRIMINATION
AND A PISSED OFF
UNINSURED AMERICAN

I am a U.S. citizen, a middle-aged woman, a wife, and mother. I have had multiple health problems for many years and am considered "disabled." Being married to a disabled husband and being disabled myself due to the chronic health conditions I've had for over 20 years, I have not been able to work outside the home enough over the past 30 years to qualify for Social Security Disability. I have no health insurance. There is no other help available for women like me to get the healthcare that we need.

And I am this close to giving up on the hope that affordable health care for all will be a reality. Why? Because

[1]   there are too many doctors with a GOD complex fighting this change with every thing that they have.

[2.] There are too many powerful drug companies spending millions of dollars to make sure that this issue stays at the bottom of the heap.

[3.] It's NEVER going to "change" as long as we have commercials on TV every 5 seconds telling us about another new drug and why we should ASK our doctor about it.

[4.] As long as the doctors and health care providers continue to receive "free" gifts . . . pens, coffee mugs, meals, trips etc., etc., from drug reps.

[5.] AND for as long as it is deemed acceptable to allow the drug companies to lobby.

Why would they not fight this, considering that they have had a monopoly on health care drug costs, and we citizens have no other choice but to purchase their medications and in the process paying for "ALL" the research, development and advertising. So why would they just roll over . . . no matter how many lives it might actually save? What's the loss of a few thousand lives per year when we're talking about billions of dollars in profits?

Have you ever wondered why we Americans pay so much more for medication than other countries pay?

Because research and development of these new drugs are very expensive . . . and because other countries (using the same drugs, from the same companies) refuse to allow the drug companies to charge the prices to their citizens that we Americans are expected to pay. So, we Americans pay most of those costs, for the world.

Being a full time mother and a wife most all my life, over the years I have heard how important these roles are . . . how that the "hand that rocks the cradle rules the world" etc., etc. And, if they added up the actual cost that it would take to pay a woman for the amount of time, effort, work, she invests in her family, (child care, cooking, cleaning etc., etc.), nobody could actually afford to pay for these services that we provide for free every single day. Yet in the Social Security system's eyes we (the very women that have stayed at home) gave everything that we have of ourselves to our families have not earned enough "real money" . . . (in my case . . . due to illness), NOT being able to hold down a "real" job for very long, over the years . . . we simply do NOT count, our life really doesn't matter. So, quite frankly, I do NOT feel and have never felt empowered as a woman or as a citizen either. Instead I have been made to feel like a second class citizen . . . a nobody.

And, it's the same for all of the millions of other uninsured Americans. The message is clear . . . none of us really matter. Why?

Because many of us do not have the required amount of hours set by Social Security in order to be considered a "real person." Nor, do we have anyone willing to stand up for us to do something that could make sure that we are treated fairly.

As I age and my health declines, the frustration has turned to trying to accept the fact that here in America there are millions of others just like me, with the numbers growing daily. We are in the same boat, and this situation may never change.

For example, recently I noticed that the insurance company paid the pharmacy 25 cents per dose for my husband's prescription; yet my prescription for the exact same medicine at the same pharmacy is 90 cents per dose because I am private pay.

That is the way it always is and always has been for all medical things for the "private pay individual". We are FORCED to pay 2, 3, 4 times and sometimes even more for the exact same services that someone with insurance coverage pays for tests, blood work, hospital and doctor visits. Where is the fairness in that for those of us that can NOT get health coverage due to our pre-existing health conditions . . . or afford the hundreds of dollars in monthly premiums, or the unrealistic (thousands of dollars) deductibles.

If you can find a company willing to insure you, how long do you think we could keep it? In my humble opinion, it feels like a form of legal discrimination, forcing us . . . the "private pay individual" . . . . to pay out of pocket so much more, for the exact same services that someone who does have coverage, has to pay. Or . . . we can do without. Not much of a choice is it?

We have no one in our corner to help bring the cost down so that we will be charged the same amount that everyone else with coverage pays. We are at the mercy of the health care provider and MUST pay whatever they tell us to pay.

As a family, we do not live above our means, yet with the cost of lab work, office visits, medication etc., and with the economy in the tank . . . living on a fixed income, paying so much more for utilities, food, gas, medication etc. than we did a year ago . . . we—like millions of other people—are finding it more difficult to make ends meet each month. The specialized care that I should have been receiving all these years and was receiving while I was insured has NOT been and is NOT a realistic option for me for the past 15 years.

Our government has one answer to my plight. For a woman my age, without enough credited hours for SS Disability: divorce. Divorce (break up our home of 19 years) and then come back and apply . . . then, "we might" be able to help you. (Might?) So we are faced with two choices . . . divorce my disabled husband and hope that the taxpayers will take care of all my needs, or continue to stay married and watch as my health continues to decline. Where are the morals that this country was founded on? Sadly, I very well may be forced to consider option number one because I need medical and financial help, and we simply can not afford all the medical tests and specialized treatments that I need without putting us farther into debt or facing bankruptcy if my health conditions continue to be left untreated.

After so many years I am exhausted and tired of hoping, of waiting "just a little while longer", and believing that help is coming for those of us that have stayed home to take care of our families. Through no choice of our own we aren't physically able to hold down a job due to chronic health issues.

The "yes we can" . . . is NEVER going to happen as long as the focus continues to remain on bailing out big business (the banks, the auto industry etc.) It's NOT our place to keep throwing endless money at them so that some of them can continue living the "high life" (bonus, spa days etc., etc.) while the uninsured American continues to struggle day after day.

If American companies can't make it work without bailout money, then they don't need to be in business. The list goes on and on . . . the utility companies expect us the consumer to foot the bill for upkeep, upgrades to their lines, and equipment, while raking in huge record profits.

So, the almighty buck continues to flow freely to other countries, to bail out big industry, and to finance wars for countries that can well afford to pay for their own protection while we Americans pay more each day for gas, heating, groceries, medicine and everything else . . . and get shafted once again.

Isn't it time instead to concentrate on the millions of other "REAL" people that are suffering day in and day out because they are not insured and do not have the means to obtain insurance? This nation that I love, the same nation founded under GOD, for the people, by the people and of the people is supposed to have the opportunity for life, liberty and the pursuit of happiness does NOT consider affordable health care as top priority but INSTEAD encourages the break down of the family unit.

Many other countries with fewer resources than our own somehow manage to insure every man, woman and child. Where are the public servants, the very ones that we elected while they promised that "Health Care for All" was indeed coming, soon? At this moment, it feels as if once again they were telling the voters what we wanted and needed to hear, in order to get elected. Those same individuals do NOT have to worry about health insurance for themselves or for their families. They can get the help they need, second opinions etc. when faced with illness, surgery etc., while the rest of us without insurance, struggle to afford basic health care needs.

It must be nice, not to have the never ending 24/7 worry of no insurance. And to have that peace of mind, knowing that you will be able to receive the care you need . . . and not have to worry constantly about it, or how you will pay the inflated cost of each and every medical service "upfront." Personally, I wouldn't know since it has been a constant worry (my reality) for so many years for me and for so many others. And it will continue to be a worry for how many more years. I do wonder how many people have been forced into bankruptcy because of medical bills. How many have died because they can't get or afford the help they need, or choose not to saddle their family with a mountain of debt? How many continue to suffer daily? The actual count would no doubt be sobering.

For those people that honestly feel that "Health Care is a Luxury and NOT a Right, I honestly don't know what to say to you except UNTIL you have actually had to walk a day/week or month in the shoes of the uninsured [the people that are sick—really sick—you don't have a clue. BUT remember this as you sit there enjoying "your Healthcare is a LUXURY NOT A RIGHT" views. You or someone you love might lose their job and after the benefits run out and the Cobra coverage has expired (if they can afford the cost of it on unemployment) you and/or they just might realize how difficult it is, living without the health care or coverage you enjoy now. We, the uninsured, do not expect a bailout or even a handout. What we do expect and deserve is to be treated fairly . . . perhaps . . . even equally to all other Americans that are fortunate enough to have either good health, or health care coverage.

Why is it too much to ask or to expect to have someone up there in Washington fighting for us?

Why is it wrong to ask for the same opportunity to receive the health care that we need at a price that we can actually afford without causing undue financial hardship on our family?

I'll continue to pray that it won't always be this way, that it will get better. But as more and more people join the ranks of the uninsured, NOTHING is going to change for the better until something major is done (and soon) to finally address and fix this issue, once and for all.

I believe that all LIFE is precious; however, the message that we (the 46 million uninsured) are getting is that LIFE is precious but ONLY if you qualify for health insurance—otherwise, not so much! I honestly don't know what the answer is but try cutting out the pork, try expecting (demanding) oil rich nations to pay their fair share for protection, stop the never-ending prescription drug commercials on TV, stop the hospitals and other health care providers from multiple billing, and cut down on the administrative costs. The mountain of paperwork that the patient has to fill out every single visit to the same doctor is not only a waste of money and time, but also contributes to the waste of our natural resources each year as well.

It amazes me that we as a nation can ALWAYS find the money to send up another space shuttle, fund wars, build bridges to nowhere and use billions of dollars for tons of other "pet" projects. YET at the very mention of "health care reform", all we hear about is "the price tag!" How much have we spent for the wars, for the space program, to bail out big business, to help other countries?

Until the healthcare issue actually touches the lives of the very people in charge of making these changes for our nation . . . . until their children, family, friends, and neighbors try to survive without the health care they need. I honestly don't think that they will fully understand the impact that it has on the millions of Americans who struggle with this every single day of their lives.

The next time you go to the doctor, hospital and pharmacy, ask what it would cost if you were private pay. Try holding your breath each month as you pick up your medication hoping that the price has not gone up once again, and having to make the decision not to take all the medications that you are suppose to be taking because you can't afford to pay for them. In other words . . . try walking that "mile" in our shoes.

HOUSING PARTNERS DISCRIMINATION AGAINST EX-OFFENDERS AND A HANDICAPPED INDIVIDUAL AT THE SAME TIME

This particular handicapped individual has lived in this Housing Partners Senior Citizens complex for over 10 years and was being taken care of by an ex-convict who had paid his debt to society. The ex-convict was convicted of a crime that had taken place twelve years before. The ex-convict served probation time, went through years of therapy, and spent four years in prison.

After paying his debt to society, the ex-convict took a job taking care of thisparticular handicapped individual for over a year. The handicapped individual trusted the ex-convict, and the two of them became good friends.

The handicapped individual trusted the ex-convict to make his doctors' appointments, clean up his apartment, do his laundry, go grocery shopping, cook his meals, and pick up his money that was managed by another friend. The handicapped individual even made the ex-convict his emergency contact person and gave him a key to the front door of his apartment.

Often times in the middle of the night the ex-convict would go to the handicapped individual's apartment because Life Alert would call the ex-convict and report that the handicapped person had fallen on the floor while trying to get in his wheel chair from the bed or while trying to get in the bed from his wheel chair. In those cases, the ex-convict would rush over to make sure that his friend was okay and to help him. This was above and beyond his job description. He did it because he cared.

In June 2009 while showing up on a routine visit, the ex-convict discovered a letter from the Housing Partners on the front door of the entrance to the apartment complex. The letter stated that the ex-convict was not allowed in the building and if seen in the building, criminal trespass charges would be brought against him.

This was devastating for the handicapped individual because now he had no other dependable and reliable personnel to attend to his needs.

What's wrong with this picture? Total discrimination against the ex-convict who had paid his debt, served his time and was working to make his life productive once again. This was also discrimination against the handicapped senior citizen by taking away his right to choose who he would have take care of him and attend to his needs as well as who he chooses to be his friend.

DISCRIMINATION AGAINST SENIOR CITIZENS

It is not uncommon for senior citizens these days to lose their homes because of the burden of having to pay insurance and taxes on their home and property. They simply can't afford it.

They worked their entire life and managed to pay off their homes and properties free and clear. After all those years of hard work, now living on a fixed income or low retirement pension, some seniors are losing their homes because they cannot afford to pay current taxes or back taxes.

I believe that the government should pass a law to protect senior citizens from being faced with this situation. Senior citizens have earned the right after all those years of paying into our system to not have to pay real estate taxes on their homes and properties.

The people in this country need to appreciate and respect our senior citizens because they are the backbone and the pride of this great nation.

DISCRIMINATION AGAINST THE MEN AND WOMEN OF THE ARMED FORCES

I am a white liberal male of Dutch, German, Irish, Algonquin, Sioux, and Cherokee Indian heritage. I do believe we are all created equal; that we should all have equal opportunities in this country and not be hated or discriminated against no matter what your race, creed, color, religion, or sexual preference. That's the bottom line.

I am an American, born and raised in this country, and I am as red, white and blue as anyone can be. I was in the United States Army, did my time in service to God and country, and received an honorable discharge. However, I am of the opinion that America needs to bring the men and women of the armed forces home.

Our military personnel are dispatched all over the world to impose America's will on others, whether invited or uninvited. Everyone does not want to be an American. Often times as a country we get involved in a pointless, meaningless war or conflict because some other country requests our assistance to fight for their cause. America is not supposed to be the world police. We have enough problems of our own in this country, and it would be high time that we—as a nation address these problems—especially the hate and discrimination issues that are out of control in this country.

In my opinion, the United States of America should become a neutral country—kind of like Switzerland—and take care of our own business at home instead of trying to solve everyone else's agendas all across the globe.

The men and women of the armed forces are not asked or even given a choice if they wish to participate in a pointless, meaningless war somewhere half way around the world. They are told, "You signed your name on the dotted line, which means good, bad or indifferent you belong to Uncle Sam." A classical case of discrimination being projected upon the men and women who joined the armed forces for all the right reasons. God bless the USA!

CONCLUSION

In closing, I think that our government—as well as each and everyone of us—should take a good look at ourselves and a good look around us to see, to know, and to ask: "Am I the problem or am I going to be the solution so we can all coexist in this country in order to make this a better place, to have a brighter future and a better tomorrow."

Yesterday is gone, tomorrow may never come. All we have is today right here and right now to make a difference.

Stop the Hate!

Lawrence J. King
Boulder, Colorado